Curriculum Visions

Move on with

Subtracting

Br... ...in Bass

Curriculum Visions

There's much more online including videos

You will find multimedia resources covering a wide range of topics at:

www.CurriculumVisions.com

CurriculumVisions is a subscription web site.

A CVP Book
Copyright © 2009 Atlantic Europe Publishing

Series Concept
Brian Knapp, BSc, PhD

Text contributed by
Brian Knapp, BSc, PhD, and Colin Bass, BSc, MA

Editors
Lorna Gilbert, Barbara Carragher, and Gillian Gatehouse

Senior Designer
Adele Humphries, BA, PGCE

Illustrations
David Woodroffe

Designed and produced by
Atlantic Europe Publishing

Printed in China by
WKT Company Ltd

Curriculum Visions Move on with Maths – Subtracting
A CIP record for this book is available from the British Library

ISBN: 978 1 86214 556 6

Picture credits
All photographs are from the Earthscape Picture Library and ShutterStock collections.

This product is manufactured from sustainable managed forests. For every tree cut down at least one more is planted.

Move on with Maths Resources CD

You will find hundreds of photocopiable word problems in the teacher's 'Move on with Maths Resources CD', which is available for separate purchase.

Look out for these sections to help you learn more about each topic:

 Remember... This provides a summary of the key concept(s) on each two-page entry. Use it to revise what you have learned.

Can you do this? These problems reinforce the concepts learned on a particular spread, and can be used to test existing knowledge.

Answers to the problems set in the 'Move on with Maths' series can be found at: **www.curriculumvisions.com/moveOnAnswers**

Place value

To make it easy for you to see exactly what we are doing, you will find coloured columns behind the numbers in all the examples on this and the following pages. This is what the colours mean:

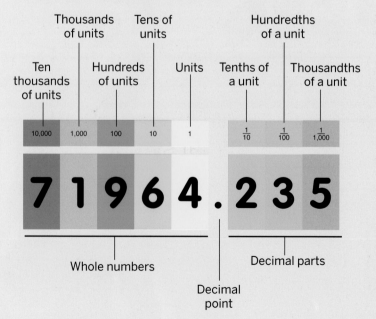

Ten thousands of units	Thousands of units	Hundreds of units	Tens of units	Units	Tenths of a unit	Hundredths of a unit	Thousandths of a unit
10,000	1,000	100	10	1	$\frac{1}{10}$	$\frac{1}{100}$	$\frac{1}{1,000}$

$$7\ 1\ 9\ 6\ 4\ .\ 2\ 3\ 5$$

Whole numbers — Decimal parts

Decimal point

Contents

Counting back

Counting back is simply moving between numbers. It is a slow but reliable way of subtracting.

We often use counting back with calendars. We may, for example, want to know how much earlier we need to post a birthday card in order for it to arrive on the actual birthday of a friend or relative.

Below is another example:

Counting back for a treat

Jane's mother thought that she would treat the children to a trip to a pantomime in the local theatre. The pantomime was to be a Christmas treat. But she found she had to book **7** days in advance. She wanted to go to the theatre on December **28th**. So she needed to count back **7** days from that day. She used her fingers, as shown on the right.

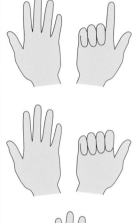

Jane's mother started on the **28th** and, using **7** fingers, she counted back the **7** days.

One day before it would be the **27th**.

Two days before it would be the **26th**.

Three days before it would be the **25th**.

Four days before it would be the **24th**.

Five days before it would be the **23rd**.

Six days before it would be the **22nd**.

Seven days before it would be the **21st**.

Counting back with longer numbers

Then Jane's mum discovered that she could get better tickets if they went to the show on the **4th** of January and booked **15** days ahead. So what would be the easiest way to do this?

She decided that it would be easier using a calendar. In this way, she soon discovered that she needed to book on the **20th** of December.

The shaded area on the calendar shows you how this was done. Remember to start on the **4th** of January and count back.

DECEMBER						
SUN	MON	TUE	WED	THU	FRI	SAT
	1	2	3	4	5	6
7	8	9	10	11	12	13
14	15	16	17	18	19	⟨20⟩
←21	←22	←23	←24	←25	←26	←27
←28	←29	←30	←31			

JANUARY						
SUN	MON	TUE	WED	THU	FRI	SAT
				←1	←2	←3
⟨4⟩	5	6	7	8	9	10
11	12	13	14	15	16	17
18	19	20	21	22	23	24
25	26	27	28	29	30	31

Counting back

John's big brother Peter has moved to Australia. Sending parcels takes three weeks. Peter's birthday is on **26th** January. When should John post him a parcel?

On the calendar above, find **26th** January. Remembering that each line of dates is a week, count upwards **3** lines, which is **3** weeks. The answer is **5th** January. Using the fact that three weeks is **21** days, check this answer by counting back as in the previous example.

≫≫ **Remember...** Counting back is a slow way of subtracting. Use it only when the numbers are complicated, such as counting back days between months.

Can you do this? Debbie usually allowed **15** days to revise for important exams. This year, her exams began on **12th** January. Using the calendar above work out when Debbie should start revising?

Write the answer on a separate piece of paper.

A ruler for subtracting

Subtracting is always the reverse of adding.

In adding, we put two collections of numbers together. We do this using a plus (+) symbol. In subtraction we take one number from another, using a minus (−) symbol.

One way to get used to subtracting is to count back using a ruler as a number line.

For example, Jose has **9** roses and wants to give **5** to his aunt for a birthday present. How many can he keep for himself?

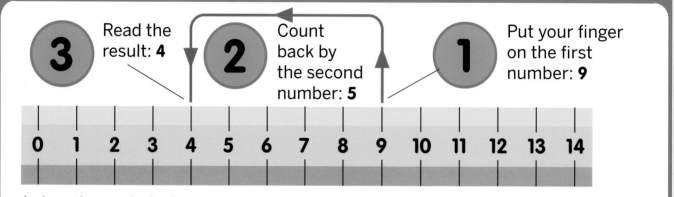

3 Read the result: **4**

2 Count back by the second number: **5**

1 Put your finger on the first number: **9**

A ruler used as a number line for counting.

So, Jose can keep **4** roses for himself.

One way of showing what we have done is to use words, for example:

Nine take away five leaves four

Or as a word equation:

Nine minus five equals four

And as a number equation this is:

$$9 - 5 = 4$$

 Remember... A ruler is useful to get you started with subtraction even if you are not good with numbers. Simply follow the three steps shown.

Here is a second example, this time with larger numbers:

Giulio wanted to finish making a model building. He was using building blocks. The instructions said he must use **28**. When he counted his stock he found he had only **12**.
How many more should he buy?

This is how Giulio worked it out using a ruler:

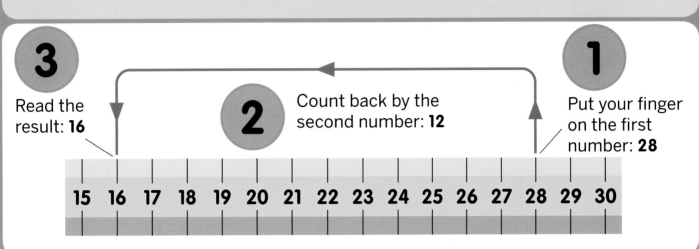

3
Read the result: **16**

2
Count back by the second number: **12**

1
Put your finger on the first number: **28**

He needed to buy **16** blocks. We can write this as:

Twenty-eight take away twelve leaves sixteen

Or as a word equation:

Twenty-eight minus twelve equals sixteen

And as a number equation it is:

$$28 - 12 = 16$$

Can you do these?
$13 - 7 = ?$
$29 - 12 = ?$
$25 - 17 = ?$

Use both the rulers to help, then write the answers out on a separate piece of paper.

Counting on to find the difference

Sometimes you need to count on to find the difference. For example, you will find it is a quick and easy way to count your change.

A book, burger and fries for Felix

Felix, who lives in San Francisco, was washing his aunt's car. When he finished, she gave him a **$10** bill. There was a book he wanted that cost **$7**, so he could buy it and also have change for a burger and fries!

He went into the shop and at the check-out Felix handed over the **$10** bill.

What the assistant did then was to add to find the difference – that is, the amount of change he was owed. The assistant did it like this:

"Seven", she said, and then she counted on as she put each dollar change in his hand: "and one is eight, and one more is nine and a final dollar makes ten".

In this way she could give the change quickly and easily and Felix could do it too – to prove that he had not been cheated!

Here is the **10** that Felix's aunt gave him:

Here are the **7** that the book cost:

Here are the **3** that Felix received in change:

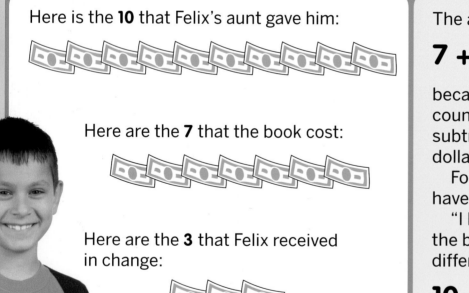

The assistant had said:

$$7 + 1 + 1 + 1 = 10$$

because she thought that counting on was easier than subtraction. So she gave **3** dollars change, one at a time.

For subtraction, she would have had to say:

"I have been given **10**, the book cost **7**, and so the difference is **3**." That is:

$$10 - 7 = 3$$

Important fact: Counting on is easier than subtraction when the numbers are small. Counting on with larger numbers is slow and carries a higher risk of making a mistake.

Find the change from a **£20** note when buying a **£16** train ticket.

The cashier counts out the change – saying **16** first, then counting on as she hands over each of the four **£1** coins...

16	17	18	19	20
	1	2	3	4

So the change is **4 pounds**.

Find the change when a **£50** note is offered for a **£39** skirt.
The cashier counts out the change – saying **39** first, then counting on as she hands over a **£1** coin and a **£10** note in change...

39   40   50

1   11   (1 + 10 = 11)

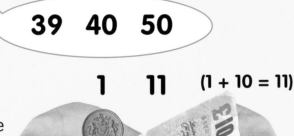

So the change is **11 pounds**.

⟫⟫⟫ **Remember...** Counting on is a useful way of subtracting when numbers are small. If you are not confident about getting the right change over a shop counter, do what shop assistants do – count on!

Can you do these? Check the change from a **£10** note for an **£8** CD.
Now suppose the CD actually cost **£7.99**. What would the change be?

Check the change from a **£50** note for a jacket costing **£37.95**.

Work the answers out on a separate piece of paper.

Subtracting rulers

If you put two rulers side by side you can use them as number lines to help you to subtract.

How far away is it?

Jemma was looking at a road map. Dad had said to her that they were going to drive between Newcastle upon Tyne and Bishop Auckland. As these were big places, they were each marked with a pin symbol on the map and the distance was marked in large writing as **28 miles**.

To get there they had to go through Durham. The distance from Newcastle to Durham was given as **17 miles**. But the map did not say how far it was between Durham and Bishop Auckland.

Jemma realised she could find the unknown distance using the rulers on her desk. What she needed to do was to take **17** from **28**. Look at the opposite page to see how she did it.

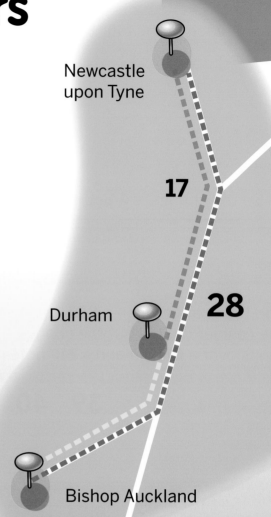

Newcastle upon Tyne

17

Durham

28

Bishop Auckland

Problem

To subtract **17** from **28** using two rulers. **28 – 17 = ?**

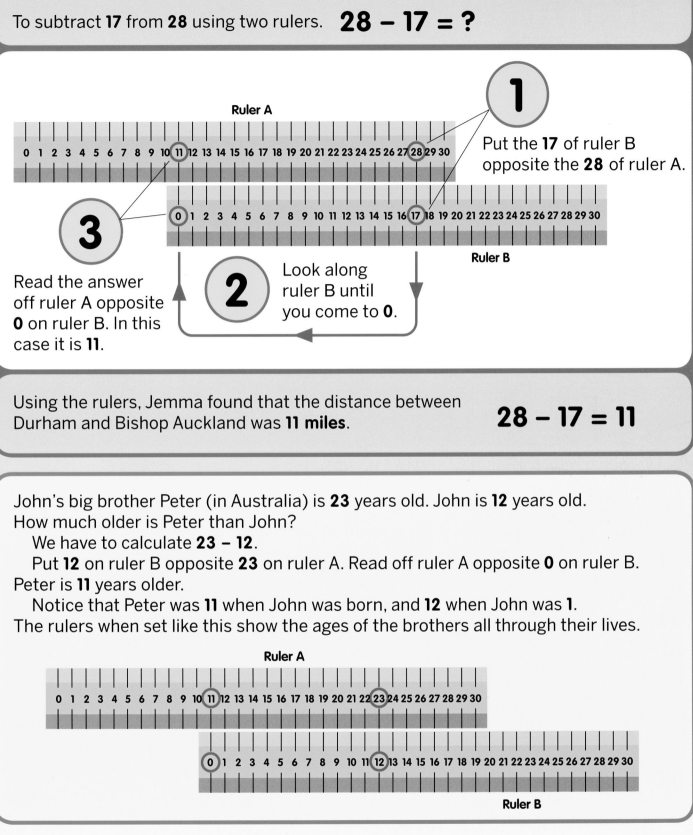

1 Put the **17** of ruler B opposite the **28** of ruler A.

2 Look along ruler B until you come to **0**.

3 Read the answer off ruler A opposite **0** on ruler B. In this case it is **11**.

Using the rulers, Jemma found that the distance between Durham and Bishop Auckland was **11 miles**.

28 – 17 = 11

John's big brother Peter (in Australia) is **23** years old. John is **12** years old. How much older is Peter than John?

We have to calculate **23 – 12**.

Put **12** on ruler B opposite **23** on ruler A. Read off ruler A opposite **0** on ruler B. Peter is **11** years older.

Notice that Peter was **11** when John was born, and **12** when John was **1**. The rulers when set like this show the ages of the brothers all through their lives.

Can you do this? Robbie's Grandpa weighs **86 kg** and would like to lose **9 kg**. What is the weight he would like to be?

Work the answer out on a separate piece of paper.

 Remember... Subtracting is the reverse of adding.

Subtracting facts

Subtracting facts are the answers we get when we take one number from another.

Here is a simple way to find out five subtraction facts.

In this case we are using a group of **5** beetles, but you could do this with a group of anything of any size.

(1) Put the beetles in a row. This simply makes it easier to see what we are doing.

(2) Separate them into two groups. Separating is a way of subtracting, as you will see on page 13.

We might start with a group of blue beetles which will be separated into two groups.

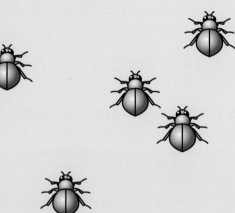

1 The blue beetles are placed in a row.

2 The beetles have now been separated out into groups. The numbers tell you how many are in each group. There are five beetles in each of the lines below.

▼ Read what has happened below. Also, notice that there are many ways to talk about subtracting.

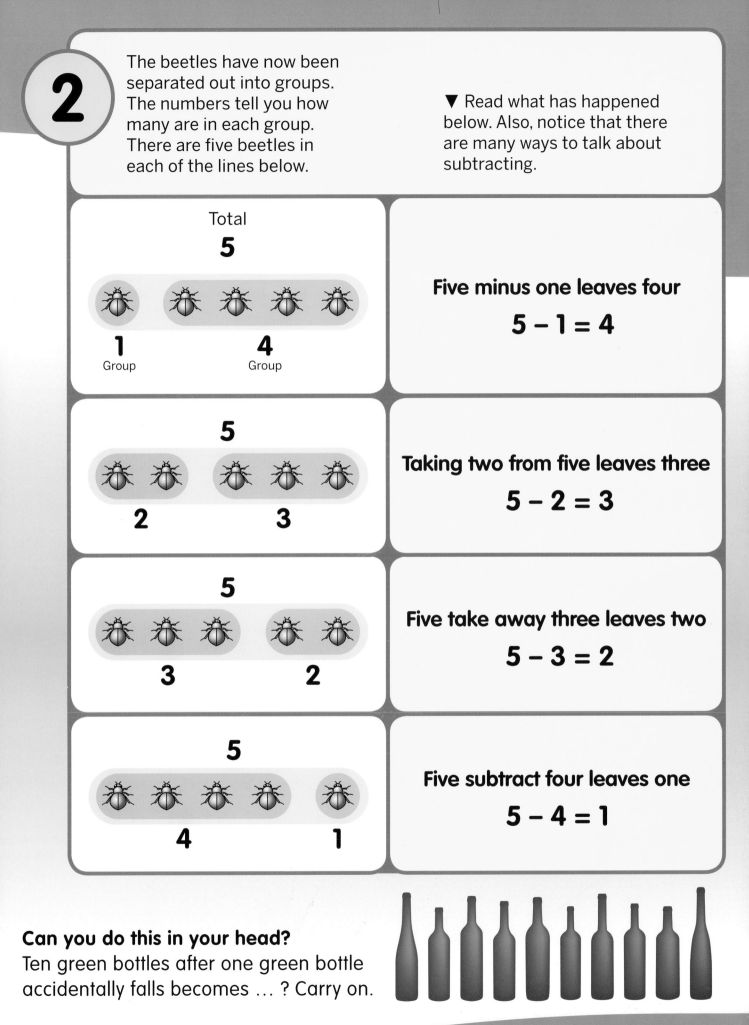

Total
5

1
Group

4
Group

Five minus one leaves four
5 – 1 = 4

5

2   **3**

Taking two from five leaves three
5 – 2 = 3

5

3   **2**

Five take away three leaves two
5 – 3 = 2

5

4   **1**

Five subtract four leaves one
5 – 4 = 1

Can you do this in your head?
Ten green bottles after one green bottle accidentally falls becomes … ? Carry on.

Pairs of subtracting facts

You can usually get two subtracting facts from each adding fact, by knowing that facts come in families.

Adding and subtracting facts go together. You can get two subtracting facts from each adding fact. This is because adding two numbers together in any order gives the same result, but the order in which you subtract numbers gives different results.

1

For example, adding fact:

6 + 3 = 9

9

6   3

2

From this we can work out that our first subtracting fact is:

9 – 6 = 3

9

6   3

3

And our second subtracting fact is:

9 – 3 = 6

9

3   6

Remember… The order in which you do your subtracting is important.

14

Here is another fact family:

5 + 2 = 7

This is our adding fact.

From this we can work out that:

7 − 2 = 5

and

7 − 5 = 2

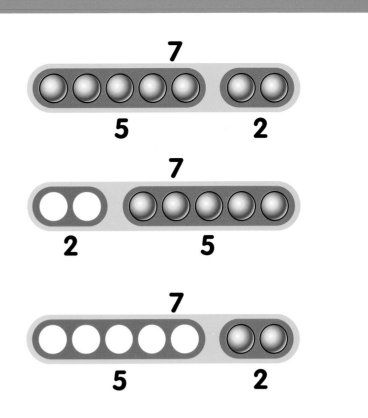

Below is a fact family with only one subtracting fact because the adding numbers are the same:

4 + 4 = 8

This is our adding fact.

From this we learn that:

8 − 4 = 4

and

8 − 4 = 4

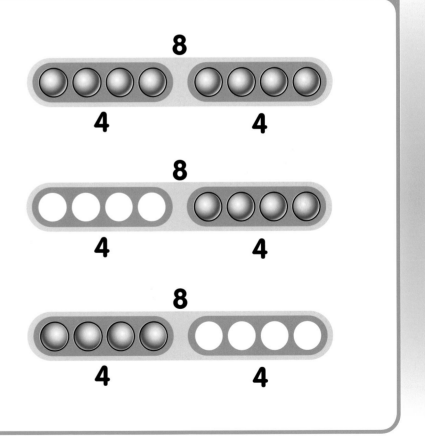

Can you do this? On a separate piece of paper, make a list of subtracting facts for ALL the pairs of numbers which add up to **8**.

Subtracting using shapes

If you are not sure how to subtract, then one way is to set out the problem as a model, using mathematical shapes.

Subtracting **4** from **9** using shapes: $9 - 4 = ?$

1 We set out **9** as units. **9** units □□□□□□□□□

2 We subtract the **4** units. **4** units □□□□

3 Then we count up the units that are left. The answer is **5** units. **5** units □□□□□□□□□

Subtracting **5** from **8** using shapes: $8 - 5 = ?$

1 We set out **8** as units. **8** units □□□□□□□□

2 We subtract the **5** units. **5** units □□□□□

3 Then we count up the units that are left. The answer is **3** units. **3** units □□□□□□□□

◄ This is a shape for **100**. You can prove this by counting up all **100** squares, or units, if you like. Some people call this shape a **flat**.

◄ This is a shape for **10**. Some people call this a **long**. Ten longs make a flat.

◄ This is a shape for **1**. It can also be called a **unit**. Ten units make a long.

Remember... The rule is to subtract units from units, tens from tens, and hundreds from hundreds. Page 18 shows another way of subtracting.

Subtracting **227** from **238** using shapes: **238 – 227 = ?**

1 Set out **238** as **2** flats, **3** longs and **8** units.

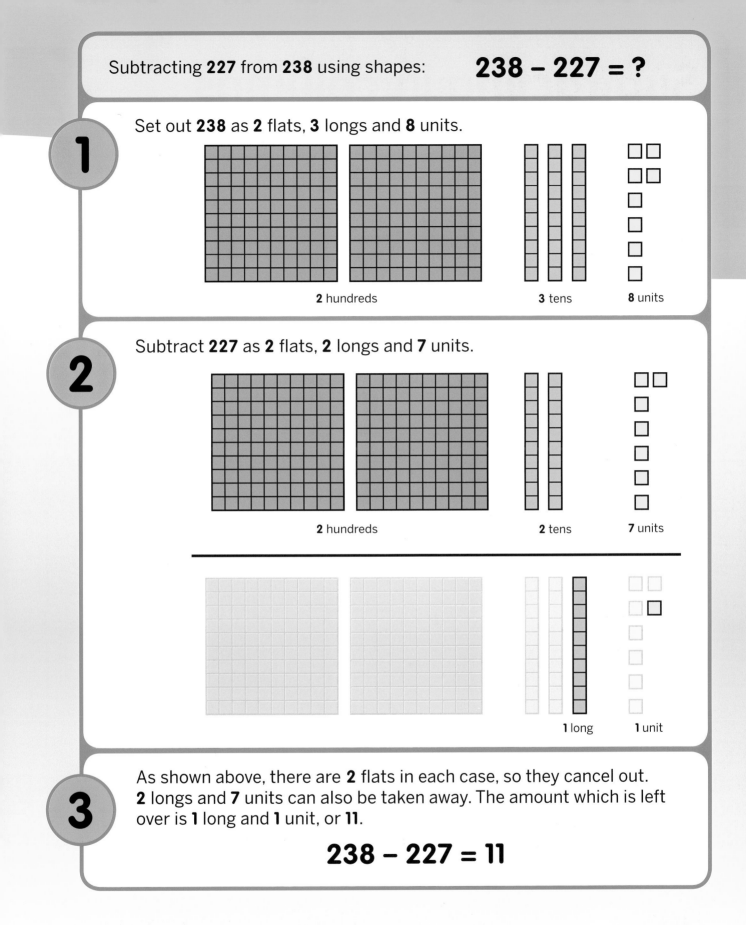

2 hundreds   3 tens   8 units

2 Subtract **227** as **2** flats, **2** longs and **7** units.

2 hundreds   2 tens   7 units

1 long   1 unit

3 As shown above, there are **2** flats in each case, so they cancel out. **2** longs and **7** units can also be taken away. The amount which is left over is **1** long and **1** unit, or **11**.

238 – 227 = 11

Can you do this? Many people find subtracting easier when they think of their "shapes" as **£1** coins.

Try it yourself for some of the examples on this page and earlier pages.

Subtracting in columns

Subtract numbers by first placing one below the other in columns.

The number you are subtracting from should be at the top, while the number you are going to subtract from it is written below.

You must also make sure that the numbers are lined up in columns. Coloured columns are used here for clarity.

What is **7 – 4** ?

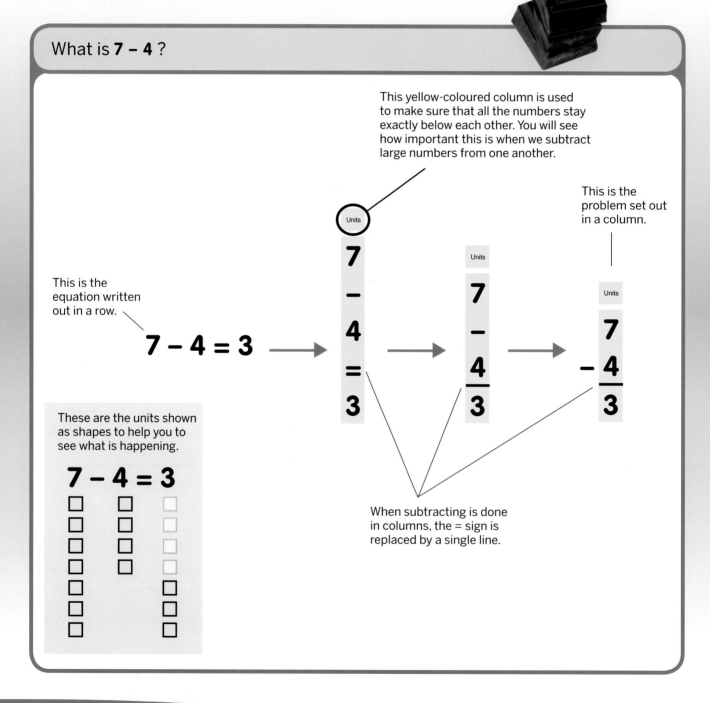

This yellow-coloured column is used to make sure that all the numbers stay exactly below each other. You will see how important this is when we subtract large numbers from one another.

This is the problem set out in a column.

This is the equation written out in a row.

$$7 - 4 = 3$$

These are the units shown as shapes to help you to see what is happening.

7 – 4 = 3

When subtracting is done in columns, the = sign is replaced by a single line.

Here are some further examples of subtracting single digits.

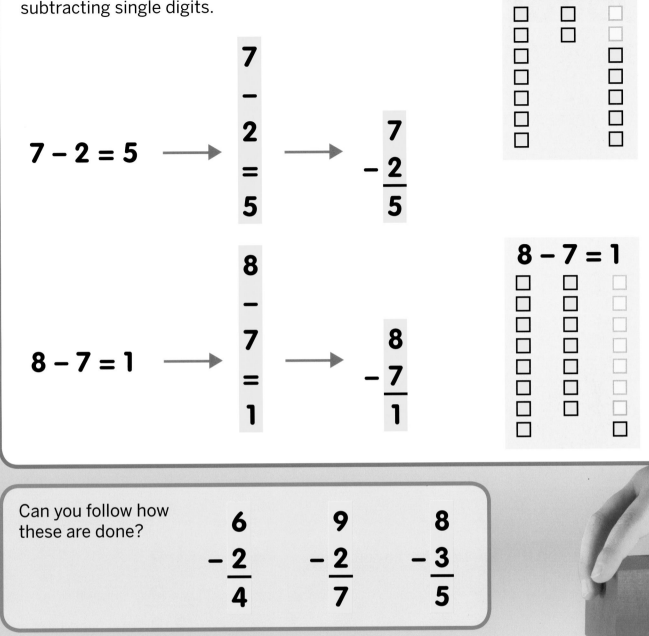

$7 - 2 = 5$

$$\begin{array}{r} 7 \\ - \ 2 \\ = \\ 5 \end{array}$$

$$\begin{array}{r} 7 \\ - \ 2 \\ \hline 5 \end{array}$$

$7 - 2 = 5$

$8 - 7 = 1$

$$\begin{array}{r} 8 \\ - \ 7 \\ = \\ 1 \end{array}$$

$$\begin{array}{r} 8 \\ - \ 7 \\ \hline 1 \end{array}$$

$8 - 7 = 1$

Can you follow how these are done?

$$\begin{array}{r} 6 \\ - \ 2 \\ \hline 4 \end{array} \qquad \begin{array}{r} 9 \\ - \ 2 \\ \hline 7 \end{array} \qquad \begin{array}{r} 8 \\ - \ 3 \\ \hline 5 \end{array}$$

⟫⟫ **Remember…** The key to success when subtracting is to keep all of your numbers in columns. This is the same idea used in adding, and it becomes very important as the numbers get bigger, as we shall soon see.

Can you do these? Write these in columns on a sheet of paper and work out the answers.

$7 - 3 = ?$

$9 - 4 = ?$

$8 - 2 = ?$

Subtracting 10 to 99

You have to use two columns to find your answer.

Put the number you are starting from on top and the one you are subtracting below it. It is very important that you line them up to the right in columns. Draw a line underneath these numbers to replace the equals symbol. Then you can subtract in each column starting on the right.

These are the tens and units shown as shapes to help you see what is happening.

16 – 5 = 11

First, let's subtract a single-digit number from a two-digit number, such as:

16 – 5 = ?

Two-digit number   Single-digit number

This is done using columns as follows:

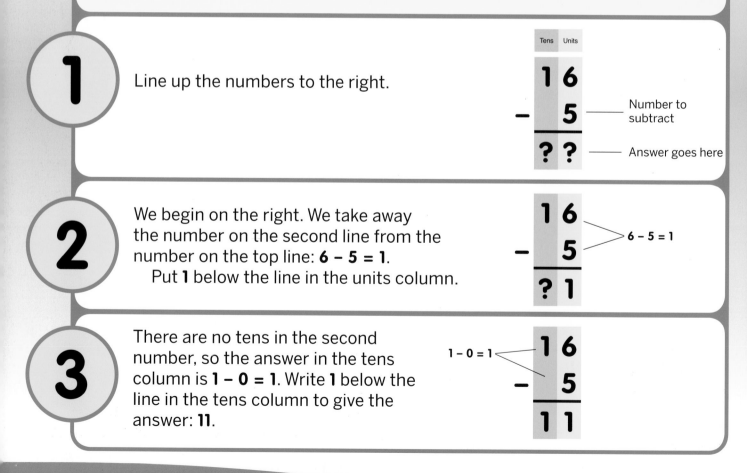

1 Line up the numbers to the right.

Tens | Units

1 6
– 5

Number to subtract

? ?

Answer goes here

2 We begin on the right. We take away the number on the second line from the number on the top line: **6 – 5 = 1**.
Put **1** below the line in the units column.

1 6
– 5

6 – 5 = 1

? 1

3 There are no tens in the second number, so the answer in the tens column is **1 – 0 = 1**. Write **1** below the line in the tens column to give the answer: **11**.

1 – 0 = 1

1 6
– 5

1 1

Subtracting 21 from 34

In this case we subtract one two-digit number from another:

34 – 21 = ?

$$34 \quad - \quad 21 \quad = \quad 13$$

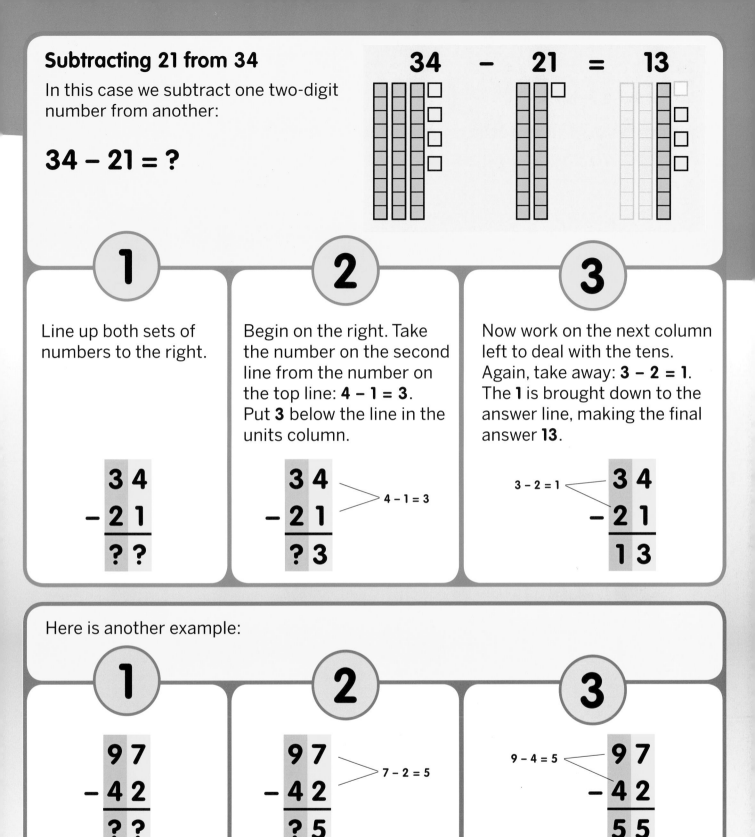

1
Line up both sets of numbers to the right.

$$\begin{array}{r} 3\,4 \\ -\,2\,1 \\ \hline ?\,? \end{array}$$

2
Begin on the right. Take the number on the second line from the number on the top line: **4 – 1 = 3**. Put **3** below the line in the units column.

$$\begin{array}{r} 3\,4 \\ -\,2\,1 \\ \hline ?\,3 \end{array}$$

$4 - 1 = 3$

3
Now work on the next column left to deal with the tens. Again, take away: **3 – 2 = 1**. The **1** is brought down to the answer line, making the final answer **13**.

$3 - 2 = 1$

$$\begin{array}{r} 3\,4 \\ -\,2\,1 \\ \hline 1\,3 \end{array}$$

Here is another example:

1

$$\begin{array}{r} 9\,7 \\ -\,4\,2 \\ \hline ?\,? \end{array}$$

2

$$\begin{array}{r} 9\,7 \\ -\,4\,2 \\ \hline ?\,5 \end{array}$$

$7 - 2 = 5$

3

$9 - 4 = 5$

$$\begin{array}{r} 9\,7 \\ -\,4\,2 \\ \hline 5\,5 \end{array}$$

Can you do these?

69 – 36 = ?

99 – 88 = ?

63 – 10 = ?

Work the answers out on a separate piece of paper.

Remember... Follow the rules. Put one number above the other, lining them up to the right using columns. Start subtracting the right-hand numbers, then move to the left, a column at a time.

Subtracting by exchanging

When the top number is smaller than the bottom number we can use a method called exchanging.

This page shows how exchanging works. The alternative 'regrouping' method is shown on pages 24 and 25. In both cases we will work out:

34 – 19 = ?

Tens of units	Units
3	**4**
– 1	**9**
?	**?**

Here is what the number **34** looks like in shapes.

Here is what the number **19** looks like in shapes.

? ?

1

To subtract **9** units from **4** units, we have added **10** units to the **4** above, making it **14**.
At the same time, we have added **1** long (**10** units) to the tens column below to balance out what we have done above.

Exchanging

2

Now we can take away **9** units from the **14** units to leave **5** units.
Then we take the **2** tens away from the **3** tens to leave one **10**.
The answer is **15**.

Pen-pal weather

Stephen, who lived in Calgary, Canada, had an email friend, Nopadom, in Bangkok, Thailand.

Stephen and Nopadom were exchanging information about the weather. In August Nopadom emailed that the temperature was **34°C**. Stephen emailed to say that in Calgary it had just reached **19°C**. So how much warmer was it in Bangkok?

$$34 - 19 = ?$$

1 Put the number you are subtracting below the one you are subtracting from, line them up to the right, and draw a line underneath them.

	Tens	Units
	3	4
−	1	9
	?	?

2 Begin in the units column: **4 − 9 = ?**

Since **9** is bigger than **4**, we need to add to the **4**. Here we exchange **10** units from the column to the left. Write a **1** beside the **4** to show that it is now **14**, and cross out the **1** in the second row of the tens column, adding **1** (1 + 1 = 2) and writing **2** to balance the **10** units we have exchanged. We can now subtract in the units column: **14 − 9 = 5**. Write the **5** below the line.

We balance the **1** ten we have exchanged by adding to the lower number in the tens column to make it **2** tens.

This is the exchanged **10** units to add to the **4**, making **14** units.

	Tens	Units
	3	¹4
−	²1̶	9
	?	5

3 Move left to the tens column.

Subtracting gives us **3 − 2 = 1**, which we write below the line.

It was **15°C** warmer in Bangkok than Calgary!

$$34 - 19 = 15$$

	Tens	Units
	3	¹4
−	²1̶	9
	1	5

Can you do these?

66 − 27 = ?

81 − 36 = ?

51 − 34 = ?

Work the answers out on a separate piece of paper.

Remember... In the exchanging method we take **1** from the column to the left to use it as **10** at the top of our working column while at the same time adding **1** to the lower number of the column to the left of it.

Subtracting by regrouping

You can subtract by the 'regrouping' method.

Regrouping is an alternative to the 'exchanging' method shown on pages 22 and 23 using the same numbers.

34 – 19 = ?

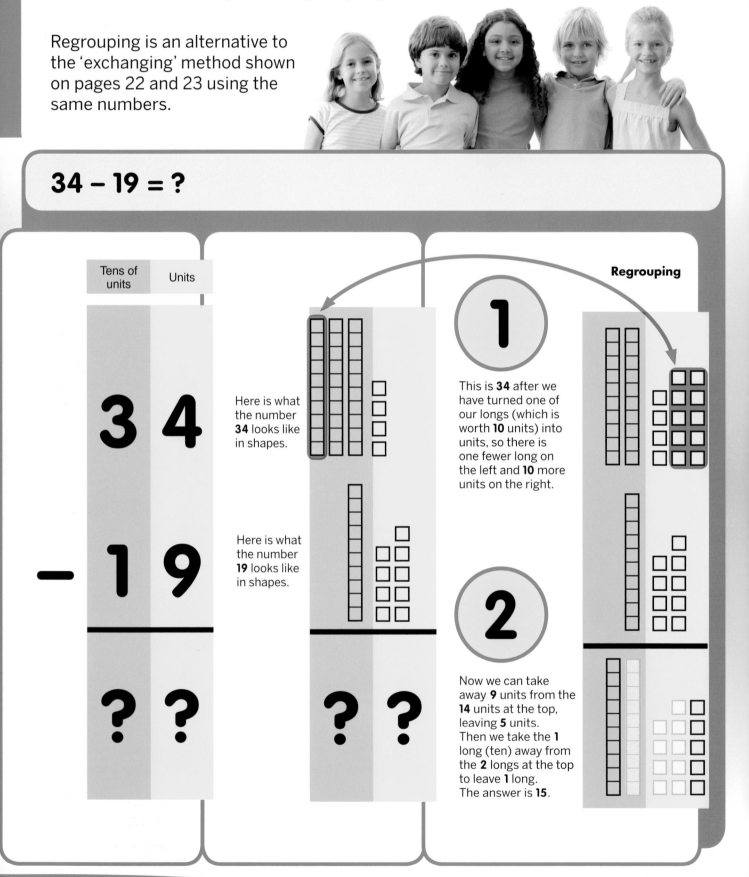

Tens of units	Units
3	**4**
– 1	**9**
?	**?**

Here is what the number **34** looks like in shapes.

Here is what the number **19** looks like in shapes.

Regrouping

1
This is **34** after we have turned one of our longs (which is worth **10** units) into units, so there is one fewer long on the left and **10** more units on the right.

2
Now we can take away **9** units from the **14** units at the top, leaving **5** units. Then we take the **1** long (ten) away from the **2** longs at the top to leave **1** long. The answer is **15**.

Changes in temperature

Juan's class was studying how much the temperature changed throughout the day. The table on the right shows the results for a school week.

This is how Juan did the one for Thursday:

$$34 - 19 = ?$$

	Highest in °C (maximum)	Lowest in °C (minimum)	Difference
Monday	25	14	11
Tuesday	31	19	12
Wednesday	26	18	8
Thursday	34	19	15
Friday	25	16	9

1 Put the number you are subtracting below the one you are subtracting from, line them up to the right in columns, and draw a line underneath them. Now subtract in each column starting on the right.

Tens   Units
```
  3 4
- 1 9
  ? ?
```

2 Start with the units column. In this case it is **4 − 9**.

Since **9** is bigger than **4**, we need to add to the **4**. Here we regroup **10** units from the tens column to the left. But because we have regrouped **1** ten from the **3** tens at the top of the column to the left, we reduce the **3** by **1** and write a **2** in its place.

We then write a **1** beside the units column to show that it is now **14** units. Now we can subtract in the units column: **14 − 9 = 5**.

After regrouping there are only **2** tens on this side.

During regrouping **1** ten is transferred to the units column as **10** units. Added to the **4** units already there, this makes a total of **14** units in the units column.

```
  ²3 ¹4
-  1  9
   ?  5
```

3 Now subtract in the tens column. Remember, we have regrouped a ten, so there are now only **2** tens in the top row of the tens column. Subtracting gives us: **2 − 1 = 1**. The temperature change on Thursday was **15°C**.

$$34 - 19 = 15$$

```
  ²3 ¹4
-  1  9
   1  5
```

Can you do these?

86 − 69 = ?

93 − 66 = ?

71 − 67 = ?

Work the answers out on a separate piece of paper.

Remember... In the regrouping method we move **1** from the top of the column to the left to use it as **10** at the top of our working column.

Subtracting large numbers

Subtracting large numbers is not difficult. But you must organise your numbers into columns.

A large number, such as **8,848**, tells you how it is made up when you say it out loud: "eight thousand (**8,000**), eight hundred (**800**) and forty (**40**) eight (**8**)". This number fits across four columns, as shown on the right.

1,000	100	10	1
8	**8**	**4**	**8**

The world's highest peaks

How much taller is Mount Everest than the tenth highest mountain, Annapurna?

We need to subtract the height of Annapurna (**8,078**) from the height of Everest (**8,848**).

8,848 – 8,078 = ?

Note: This calculation is done using the regrouping method (see page 24).

	Mountain	Height (metres)
1	Everest	**8,848**
2	K-2	**8,611**
3	Kanchenjunga	**8,598**
4	Lhotse	**8,516**
5	Makalu	**8,481**
6	Cho Oyu	**8,201**
7	Dhaulagiri	**8,172**
8	Manaslu	**8,156**
9	Nanga Parbat	**8,126**
10	Annapurna	**8,078**

1

Put the number you are subtracting below the one you are subtracting from, line them up to the right in columns, and draw a line underneath them. Now subtract in each column starting on the right.

Start with units: **8 – 8 = 0**. Write the answer below the line.

```
  8 8 4 8
– 8 0 7 8
  ? ? ? 0
```

2

Now subtract the tens.
 Subtract the next column to the left. As the **4** at the top is less than **7**, we need to regroup **100** from the hundreds column. As we are working with tens, the regrouping gives us **10** tens and the **4** tens we already have. The subtraction is now: **14 − 7 = 7**.

$$
\begin{array}{r}
8\,{}^{7}8\,{}^{1}4\,8 \\
-\ 8\,0\,7\,8 \\
\hline
?\,?\,7\,0
\end{array}
$$

3

Now subtract the next column to the left. This is the hundreds column. Remembering that as we regrouped from this column in step 2, we have reduced the **8** at the top to **7**. The subtraction is now: **7 − 0 = 7**.

$$
\begin{array}{r}
8\,{}^{7}8\,{}^{1}4\,8 \\
-\ 8\,0\,7\,8 \\
\hline
7\,7\,0
\end{array}
$$

4

Now subtract thousands.
 Subtract the next column to the left. This is the thousands column.
 The subtraction is: **8 − 8 = 0**.
 When a zero is the first number, we normally leave it out and so in this case we are left with an answer of **770**.

$$
\begin{array}{r}
8\,{}^{7}8\,{}^{1}4\,8 \\
-\ 8\,0\,7\,8 \\
\hline
7\,7\,0
\end{array}
$$

By subtracting, we know that Everest is **770** metres higher than the tenth highest mountain, Annapurna.

Can you do this?
Why not practise finding the difference in height of some of the other mountains in the table using the exchanging method and the regrouping method, to see which method you like best?

>>> **Remember…** There is no real difference between subtracting with big or small numbers. Just line the numbers up to the right and subtract starting from the right. You can use either exchanging or regrouping.

Subtracting numbers with zeros

When you subtract, you treat a zero just like any other number.

How far have we travelled?

Laura and Luke were writing out their holiday diaries. They wrote down the total miles each morning, so they could work out later how far they travelled each day. This is what they recorded for the four days of their mini-break:

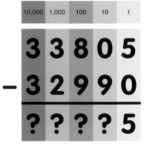

32990 miles

33805 miles

	The morning of the first day, just before they started (Day 1).	The morning of Day 2, just before they started.	The morning of Day 3, just before they started.	The morning of Day 4, back home.
Distance	**32,990**	**33,124**	**33,492**	**33,805**

To find out how far they had driven over the whole trip, they had to subtract the distance at the start of Day 4 from the distance at the start of Day 1. This is what they did:

$$33,805 - 32,990 = ?$$

1 As before, put the number you are subtracting below the one you are subtracting from. Line them up to the right in columns. You do not need to put commas in your work when subtracting.
Subtract the right-hand column (units) first: **5 – 0 = 5**.

10,000	1,000	100	10	1
3	3	8	0	5

−
| 3 | 2 | 9 | 9 | 0 |

? ? ? ? 5

Note: This calculation is done using the exchanging method. See page 22.

2 Now subtract in the next column to the left, the tens column.
In this case it is **0 – 9**, which won't go. Exchange **1** from the hundreds column to make **10** tens. The subtraction is now: **10 – 9 = 1**.

3 3 8 0¹ 5

−
3 2 9 ₁₀9̷ 0

? ? ? 1 5

3

Now subtract in the hundreds column.

The lower number is actually **10** because we had to exchange a ten in step **2**.

8 – 10 won't go. Exchange **1** from the thousands column to add to the **8** and make **18** hundreds at the top of the hundreds column. The subtraction is now: **18 – 10 = 8**.

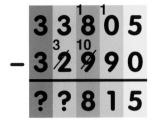

4

Move left to the thousands column. Remember we have exchanged a thousand; the subtraction is now: **3 – 3 = 0**.

Subtract the next column to the left. This is the tens of thousands column. The subtraction is again: **3 – 3 = 0**.

We do not write the zeros when they occur at the start of a number, which means that the distance was **815**.

33,805 – 32,990 = 815

The twins flew from Los Angeles to Perth, Australia, with a stopover in Sydney, Australia. In Perth they learned they had flown **9,604** miles in all, and that it would be **2,031** miles back to Sydney.

Tired of flying, they wanted to know how far it would be home to Los Angeles from Sydney.

It would be another **7,573** miles!

Can you do this?

Which day of their holiday did Laura and Luke travel farthest? How far was it?

Give your answers on a separate piece of paper.

Remember... How to work with zeros. When you are subtracting with zeros in the top line, unless the number below it is also zero, you will need to carry a '**1**' across. Which means **0** becomes **10**.

Subtracting decimal numbers

Decimals show whole numbers and parts of numbers separated by a decimal point (full stop).

A full stop is placed after the units, so that we will know which one it is. The full stop is called a decimal point.

Just as with whole numbers, which have the smallest on the right and the largest on the left, so every number to the right of the decimal point has a value ten times smaller than its left-hand neighbour. The further it is to the right, the smaller it is. Numbers below units are described as tenths, hundredths, thousandths and so on.

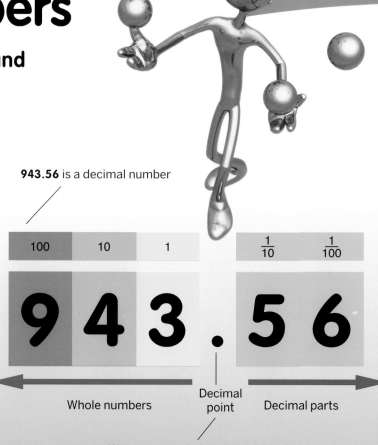

943.56 is a decimal number

100	10	1		$\frac{1}{10}$	$\frac{1}{100}$

$$9\ 4\ 3\ .\ 5\ 6$$

Whole numbers   Decimal point   Decimal parts

We <u>separate</u> whole numbers from parts of whole numbers using a decimal point

Subtracting with decimals

Subtracting with decimals is just the same as subtracting with whole numbers. Here are the stages in subtracting the decimal number **37.9** from another decimal number, **943.56**:

$$943.56 - 37.9 = ?$$

Remember... When subtracting decimals, line up the numbers about the decimal point.

1 Put the number you are subtracting below the one you are subtracting from, making sure the decimal point lines up. If the numbers have an unequal number of decimals, write zeros in the empty columns. In this case a zero (**0**) has been added to the **37.9** to make it **37.90**.

Line up the numbers using the decimal point.

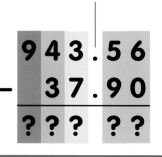

```
   9 4 3 . 5 6
 -   3 7 . 9 0
 ─────────────
   ? ? ? . ? ?
```

2 Now start subtracting from the right (the hundredths column): **6 – 0 = 6**. Write this below the line in the hundredths column.

```
  9 4 3 . 5 6
–   3 7 . 9 0
  ? ? ?   ? 6
```

3 In the next column (tenths), **5 – 9** won't go, so exchange **1** from the column to the left and increase the bottom number by **1**. Now it is: **15 – 9 = 6**.

```
  9 4 3 .¹5 6
–   3 ₈7 . 9 0
  ? ? ?   6 6
```

4 In the next column (units), **3 – 8** (**7** + the exchanged **1**) won't go, so exchange again from the left: **13 – 8 = 5**.

```
  9 4 ¹3 .¹5 6
–   ₄3 ₈7 . 9 0
  ? ?   5   6 6
```

5 In the next column (tens), **4 – 4** (**3** + the exchanged **1**) = **0**.

```
  9 4 ¹3 .¹5 6
–   ₄3 ₈7 . 9 0
  ? 0   5   6 6
```

6 The last step is **9 – 0 = 9**.

```
  9 4 ¹3 .¹5 6
–   ₄3 ₈7 . 9 0
  9 0   5   6 6
```

7 Put a decimal point in the answer exactly below the other decimal points. This gives the final answer, which is **905.66**.

```
  9 4 ¹3 .¹5 6
–   ₄3 ₈7 . 9 0
  9 0 5 . 6 6
```

Can you do this? 3.017 – 1.2 = ?

Work the answer out on a separate piece of paper.

Subtracting in your head

Any good sportsperson can keep score in their head.

Many sports and games need quick and accurate use of mathematics. A good example of this is the traditional English game of darts which is now played worldwide.

Each player has three darts, like the ones shown here. The target is a dartboard marked off in numbered zones.
The players take turns standing a fixed distance from the board and throwing their darts into it.

Usually, each player starts with a score of **501**. The score for each three darts is added up and then the total is subtracted from the remaining score. The first one to reach zero wins.

In this example we show you how the players used a variety of methods to subtract quickly. Check them for yourself to see which one suits you best.

The picture below shows the points system used in darts.

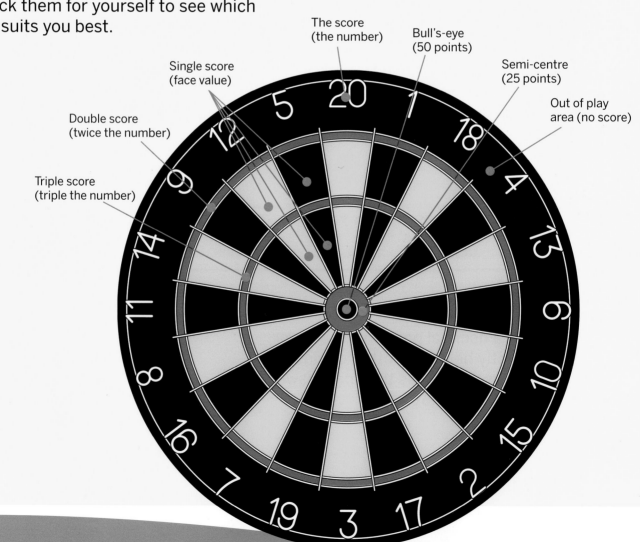

The score (the number)

Bull's-eye (50 points)

Semi-centre (25 points)

Out of play area (no score)

Single score (face value)

Double score (twice the number)

Triple score (triple the number)

Sara

Starting score: **501**

First throw gets a total of: **119**

So the score left is:

501 − 119 = 382

We can do this by counting up:
119 + 80 = 199; **199 + 2 = 201**;
201 + 300 = 501.

By this method the answer is:
80 + 2 + 300 = 382

Second throw gets a score of: **129**

382 − 129 = 253

Do this subtraction by counting up:
129 + 50 = 179; **179 + 3 = 182**;
182 + 200 = 382.

By this method the answer is:
50 + 3 + 200 = 253

Third throw gets a score of: **95**

253 − 95 = 158

Do this subtraction by subtracting
100 and adding back **5**!
(−100 + 5 = −95)
253 − 100 = 153; **153 + 5 = 158**.

Fourth throw gets a score of: **158**

158 − 158 = 0

So Sara wins!

Can you do these in your head?
143 − 38 = ?
143 − 78 = ?

Nasim

Starting score: **501**

First throw gets a total of: **77**

So the score left is:

501 − 77 = 424

We can do this subtracting using the exchanging method:

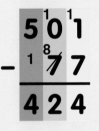

Second throw gets a score of: **153**

424 − 153 = 271

Do this subtraction by counting up:
153 + 1 = 154; **154 + 70 = 224**;
224 + 200 = 424

By this method the answer is:
1 + 70 + 200 = 271

Third throw gets a score of: **128**

271 − 128 = 143

(Do this subtraction by taking off
130 and adding back **2**!)
271 − 130 = 141; **141 + 2 = 143**

But Sara has already won by getting the exact score with her fourth throw.

 Remember... There are many ways of subtracting. Learn to use the one that works most easily for the numbers.

Subtracting and minus numbers

Sometimes the number you are subtracting from is smaller than the number you are subtracting.

Subtracting above zero

For an ordinary subtraction where the number you are subtracting from is bigger than the number you are subtracting the answer is above zero (**0**). This can be shown using a number line.

For example: **5 – 3 = ?**

5 is your starting number and **3** is your journey along the number line. Use the following steps:

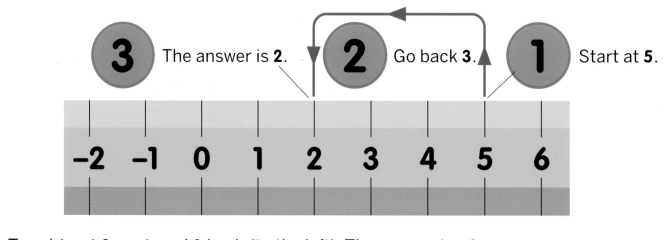

To subtract **3**, we travel **3** back (to the left). The answer is **+2**, normally just written as '**2**'.

Here's another example: **6 – 5 = 1**

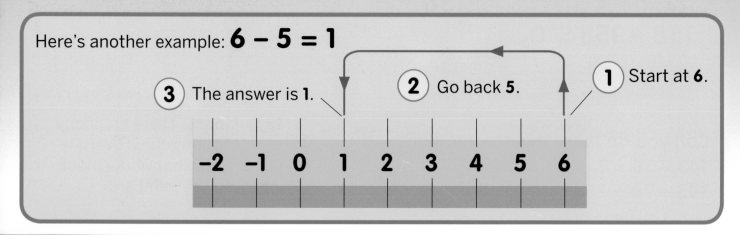

Subtracting below zero

When the number you are subtracting from is smaller than the number you are subtracting, the answer is below zero. This can also be shown using a ruler.

For example: **3 – 5 = ?**

Use the number line again: **3** is your starting number and **5** is your journey along the ruler. Use the following steps:

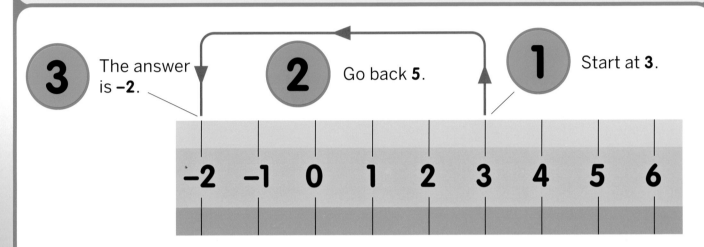

To subtract **5**, we travel **5** to the left. The answer is **–2**, which we would normally say as 'minus **2**'.

This number is below zero and, like all numbers below zero, is called a minus number. See page 36 for what we mean when subtracting across zero.

Here's another example: **4 – 5 = –1**

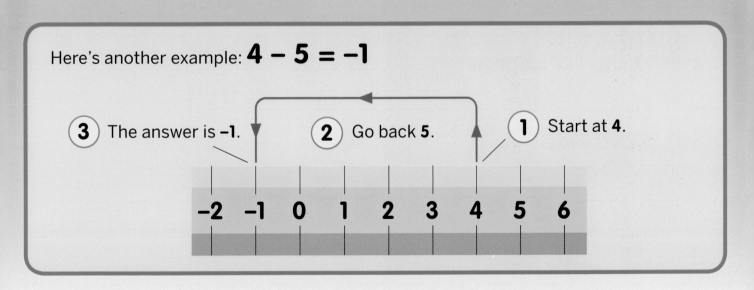

Can you do these?

1 – 3 = ?

6 – 7 = ?

Use the ruler above to help, then write the answers out on a separate piece of paper.

 Remember… Some subtractions can give minus numbers. Then you must use a minus sign immediately in front of the number.

Subtracting across zero

A minus number is a number with a minus sign in front of it.

There are many cases when people need to work with minus numbers. Here is an example.

Falling levels

Reservoirs are used to store water from rivers. Engineers know how much water they want to store in a reservoir. This can be thought of as the normal level. The level of water in a reservoir can be measured with a rod placed beside the dam.

Normal is marked as zero; a scale can then be marked up and down from normal. Numbers above normal are plus numbers; numbers below normal are minus numbers.

At the end of a rainy period an engineer measured the water level in their reservoir as **1.0** metres above normal; but as there was no more rain, he had to release some of the water to keep the river flowing. By the end of a week the water level had fallen to **0.9** metres above normal. How much had the water level fallen?

$$1.0 - 0.9 = ?$$

The answer, **0.1** metres, is shown below.

But at the end of eight weeks without rain, the level of the reservoir had fallen to below normal. The engineers read this as **−2** metres as it was **2** metres below zero. How much had the water level fallen altogether?

To find out, the engineer had to subtract with a minus number. The minus number is shown in brackets so that you can see it clearly:

$$1 - (-2) = ?$$

First, from the picture of the measuring gauge on the right, you can see the answer must be **3** metres.

Subtracting a minus number is the same as adding a plus number:

$$1 - (-2) = 1 + 2 = 3$$

The same rule works for decimal numbers. Suppose the water level had fallen from **1.5** metres to **−2.5** metres. The fall in the water level would be worked out as:

$$1.5 - (-2.5) = 1.5 + 2.5 = 4$$

You can check this on the gauge, too.

The ancient Jewish fortress of Masada stands on a barren rock **30 m** above sea level. The Judean desert to the west is **60 m** below sea level. (Much of Israel is below the level of the Mediterranean Sea.) But to the east, the cliffs fall straight down from Masada to the Dead Sea, **420 m** below sea level and the lowest point on Earth. The natural approaches to the cliff top are very difficult.

How high are the cliffs between Masada and the surrounding desert?

$$30 - (-60) = 90 \text{ metres}$$

How high are the cliffs between Masada and the Dead Sea?

$$30 - (-420) = 450 \text{ metres}$$

How far is the Dead Sea below the general level of the Judean Desert?

$$-60 - (-420) = 420 - 60$$
$$= 360 \text{ metres}$$

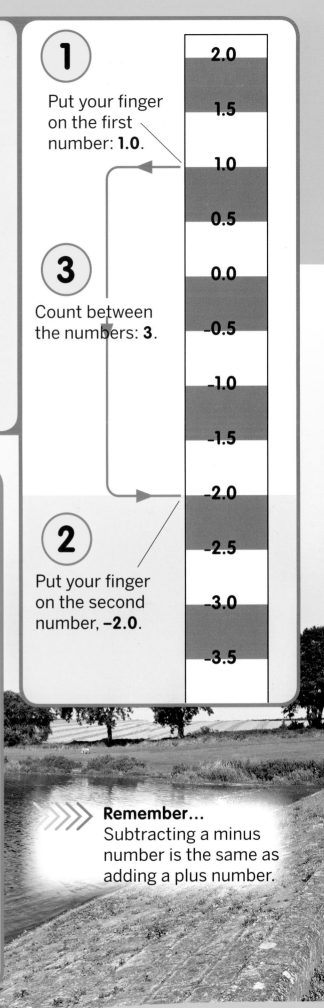

1 Put your finger on the first number: **1.0**.

3 Count between the numbers: **3**.

2 Put your finger on the second number, **−2.0**.

> **Remember…** Subtracting a minus number is the same as adding a plus number.

2.0
1.5
1.0
0.5
0.0
-0.5
-1.0
-1.5
-2.0
-2.5
-3.0
-3.5

Solving equations

By putting word problems into numbers (equations), it can be easier to see the answer.

Freda had some computer games. She added **5** more games, and then she had **14**. How many games did she start with?
   Freda's problem is:

$$\boxed{?} + 5 = 14$$

Harry had **14** games but gave some away until he had only **5** left. How many did he give away?
   Harry's problem is:

$$14 - \boxed{?} = 5$$

Inderjit had **14** computer games. He put all his 'driving games' to one side and was left with **5** games. How many driving games did he have?
   Inderjit's problem is:

14 – driving games = 5

Lai Tun Park has a collection of **14** computer games. He took all the 'platform games' out, but he forgot to count how many of them there were. Later, all the platform games were stolen. Lai Tun counted that he had **5** games remaining. How many had been stolen?
   Lai Tun Park's problem is:

14 – stolen games = 5

Although the questions above may all appear to be different, by setting them out as an equation, we discover they are all the same. They can all be represented by the equation:

$$14 - 5 = \boxed{?}$$

and the value of $\boxed{?}$ is always **9**. You can see why opposite.

To solve all of these equations, we need to remember that an equation still balances if we add the same number to each side or if we subtract the same number from each side.

To solve Freda's problem, subtract **5** from each side of the equation:

$$\boxed{?} + 5 - 5 = 14 - 5$$
$$\boxed{?} = 14 - 5$$
$$\boxed{?} = 9$$

To solve Harry's problem, add $\boxed{?}$ to both sides:

$$14 - \boxed{?} + \boxed{?} = 5 + \boxed{?}$$
$$14 = 5 + \boxed{?}$$

Now subtract **5** from both sides:

$$14 - 5 = \boxed{?}$$
$$9 = \boxed{?}$$

To solve Inderjit and Lai Tun Park's problems, add either 'driving games' (dg) or 'stolen games' (sg) to both sides. For example:

$$14 - dg + dg = 5 + dg$$
$$14 = 5 + dg$$

Now take **5** from both sides:

$$14 - 5 = dg$$
$$9 = dg$$

 Remember… If we do the same thing to both sides of an equation, it remains balanced.

Can you do this?
Harbajan spent **£14** on a train home, and arrived with only **£5** left. How much did he have before?

Write this problem out as an equation on a separate piece of paper, then work out the answer.

What symbols mean

Here is a list of the common maths symbols together with an example of how they are used.

+ The symbol for adding. We say it 'plus'. In Latin plus means 'more'.

− Between two numbers this symbol means 'subtract' or 'minus'. In front of one number it means the number is a minus number. In Latin minus means 'less'.

= The symbol for equals. We say it 'equals' or 'makes'. It comes from a Latin word meaning 'level' because weighing scales are level when the amounts on each side are equal.

$$(8 + 9 - 3) \times \frac{2}{5} = 5.6$$

( ) The symbols for brackets. You do everything inside the brackets first. Brackets always occur in pairs.

✕ The symbol for multiplying. We say it 'multiplied by' or 'times'.

—, **/** and **÷** Three symbols for dividing. We say it 'divided by'. A pair of numbers above and below a **/** or **—** make a fraction, so $^2/_5$ or $\frac{2}{5}$ is the fraction two-fifths.

. This is a decimal point. It is a dot written after the units when a number contains parts of a unit as well as whole numbers. This is the decimal number five point six.

Index